Over By the Lake
LAKE ZURICH, ILLINOIS, IN THE MIDDLE OF THE 20th CENTURY

Paul Runkel

ISBN: 1-945493-05-4
ISBN-13: 978-1-945493-05-8

TABLE OF CONTENTS

WITH SPECIAL THANKS TO:

Dick Price, of the Ela Historical Society And Museum,
Linda Runkel,
And Lori Shula.

PROLOGUE

In the quarter- century - from 1930 to 1955, Lake Zurich survived a world wide depression, World War II and became one of the many small US towns to have a TV in almost every home. President Roosevelt was elected to his first of four terms , Elvis Presley was born and Babe Ruth died.

"What a wonderful place to grow up – We were lucky to live in that place and time." That was one of my classmates, Bob Anson, speaking at our 50th class reunion. We were asked to make any remarks if we felt like it. Bob's comments stuck with me and I finally had to write a book about them.

This is that book. It is a collection of stories about a small American town, Lake Zurich, Illinois, and the people who lived and worked there in the 1940s and 50s. Lake Zurich was a microcosm of a much larger town, a community of athletes, talented business men, summer theater, inventors and members of Tom Brokaw's greatest generation.

The book is a collection of stories about these people. The specific stories were selected for the book based on how well they represented the positive attributes of the community and the availability of information about them. There is no intent to suggest these folks were the most important people in the town, they just happened to be representative of those people who lived in Lake Zurich and the surrounding communities .

Sports and theater were provided on the local level, usually by the towns people. Much of it involved the summer theater and the town baseball team. The town and high school baseball teams featured solid pitching by Eddie and Donnie Prouty, George Schwarz and Jim Obenauf. The summer theater helped to begin the careers of Geraldine Paige and Harvey Korman. This was a generation who survived the depression and then went to war. So, people made do with what was available. My dad's planning center, for example, was an old shack previously used as an outhouse.

The people believed in God and went to church. Well, most of the time, anyway. One person, your author, believes he received a message about golf from a friend in heaven. I know this is unlikely, but I like to consider the possibility. You can read the story of Guy Farman and the birdies and then make your own decision.

We had role models. Harriet Jaquat and Mel Eide, teachers at Ela-Vernon High School, who not only taught various subjects, they also motivated us to do our homework and plan ahead. In fact most of the Ela-Vernon teachers emphasized these techniques. We would use them all of our lives. Harold Giese and his fellow POWs showed spirit and a desire to survive no matter their situation. Jim Obenauf had learned the procedures to use when his aircraft was in trouble. He took the necessary steps to land the plane safely. Then there were the "Charlies", Mionske and Erickson, men who believed in hard work and creativity.

Lake Zurich was not unique in providing positive learning experiences for the next generation. The town did, however, have an unusually wide ranging mix of activities.

The Lake

PAUL RUNKEL

THE LAKE

Lakes are beautiful and always add to the local scenery. On a warm summer evening, watching the sun slip below the lake's horizon was a thing of beauty. Later on in the evening when the noise of the day's activity had slowed to a whisper, conversation floated across the water from boats and the land on the other side of the lake. These nights provided some of my most vivid memories.

Lakes are important geographical references. When Chicago people refer to the "the lake" they, of course, mean Lake Michigan. In Lake Zurich "the lake" means the body of water surrounded by Route 22, Rand Road, and Old Rand Road. We had an additional location reference, the seawall. The seawall was a concrete structure about 127 feet long on the south east side of the lake, just opposite where route 22 passed closest to the water, before it swung east toward the main business district. The wall had four openings so people could gain access to the water.

The summer theater was on the south east side of the lake. So, when you told people the theater was across from the seawall, they knew the theater's exact location. Farman's Hotel and Restaurant was on Route 22 about a block east of the seawall. Chicago slang would have been, "It's at the seawall over by dere". In Lake Zurich it was simply, "It's over by the lake" or It's over by the seawall.

Fishing was a major summer activity. There always seemed to be ten to twenty fishing boats on the lake. Apparently, the fishing was pretty good. There was always a rumor that the center of the lake had a small section 80 feet deep, populated with large bass, some as long as two or three feet. I never saw bass that large. There also was sighting of several really long black fish - as long as one half the length of a row boat. I never saw any large black fish either. I didn't want to see any fish that long; a fish almost my size is scary! However, these sightings were never confirmed.

I wasn't allowed to go out that far on to the lake, and I wasn't all that unhappy about it. So I fished along the shoreline where I occasionally saw one foot long carp and tried to catch them using several fancy lures I received for my birthday. The lures were replicas of several inch long fish

5

with hooks hanging from their underbelly. One day I saw a 15 to 20 inch long carp coming in close to shore. I made a perfect cast landing the lure right in front of the carp's nose. It looked at the lure, then at me, wiggled its tail and moved on for something more appetizing. So much for the fancy lure. Actually, the only fish I ever caught were small blue gills using a bobber and worm.

Swimming was another favorite lake activity. We always brought along a tire inner tube. If we got tired, we would float along on the tube. Most of us became decent swimmers because we spent so much time in the water.

Canoe sailing was popular on a warm summer day. People would attach a sail to their canoe and glide over the lake's surface for most of a day. When the wind picked up, the sailor had all he could do to hold the boat on the desired line. Many new sailors found themselves on the wrong side of the lake.

In the winter, residents continued to use the lake for fun activities. Some folks drove their cars out on to the ice and went fishing. They would park, cut a hole in the ice and drop a line through the hole. They could sit in their cars for protection from the winter wind. There were usually several cars on the lake at once on a week end day; the fishing must have been good. As kids we skated and played ice hockey. We never had more than four or five kids, so the teams were small (two or three kids at the most).

My grandpa was the "official tester" of the ice's thickness. He would test the ice in several places. I think it had to be five to ten inches thick before he said it was safe for skating. When it was safe he would don his skates and take a "ceremonial skate" along the ice in front of our home and the homes of several neighbors. He always wore a suit and tie for the ceremonial skate.

The ice would eventually be thick enough to support a small single engine airplane. We know this because during the cold winter months, small planes landed on the lake, checked out the fishing, and flew away to return another day.

My dad and several friends played a game they called ice golf. They used golf balls painted red. The game only lasted for a couple holes because the ball would hit the ice and role forever. The players were quickly exhausted after chasing those red balls around half the lake.

There is something about water that speaks of romance. For a number of years, there was a restaurant at the corner of Route 12 and Old Rand Road. It had a dance floor overlooking the lake. On special occasions, a band performed and diners would dance after dinner. I was there with my parents one summer evening when they danced to a romantic tune. When everyone danced, the cigarette smoke declined to a minimum which made me more comfortable. The setting including floor to ceiling windows overlooking the lake, the people swaying back and forth, and the enchanting music left an impression on my ten year old brain – one I've never forgotten. My parents looked at each other in a way I never noticed before. I was a little embarrassed, then I got lost in the moment. I think we had just seen the Humphrey Bogart movie, "Casablanca", because I said to my mother in my best Bogart snarl as she and my dad came off the dance floor, "What's a young chick like you doing in a dive like this"? She laughed and I sipped my drink … (it was a Coke).

What does a lake bring to a locality? It brings sports, beauty and romance. It also provides a constant geographical reference enabling you to describe the location of homes, businesses and other landmarks. If you lived in Lake Zurich in the mid 20th century, you'll remember there was a hotdog stand on Route 22 serving several types of sandwiches and soda. You don't remember it ? Well it was over by the lake, just at the north end of the seawall.

PAUL RUNKEL

Planning, Gambling, and Drinking

We take a look at Webb Runkel's weekly planning sessions, what happens when business owners use gambling to increase their business, and what can happen when people drink too much.

PAUL RUNKEL

14 TAVERNS AND AN OUTHOUSE

On Sunday mornings, my dad spent some time in an old wooden outhouse on the rear of our property. He read the paper and planned his upcoming work week in the solitude of this old, wooden structure. The outhouse hadn't been used for its original purpose in 20 years. It was now just an old wooden shack with a bench in it. It sat several hundred feet to the rear of our house, and was surrounded by 15 foot thick bushes. The bushes were so thick you wouldn't know the shack was there until you got close to the structure.

My dad spent an hour or so in that shack every Sunday morning. He was an insurance agent whose main customers resided in Lake Zurich. A number of them owned taverns or establishments that had liquor licenses. Anyone with a liquor license had to carry personal liability insurance. This was required by a law, called the "Dram Shop Act."

In 1951 small town taverns were the "Facebook" of that era. They were often social clubs providing a place for men to gather and greet new friends and communicate with old ones. Some women also frequented the bars, but some townsfolk did not approve of this.

One Sunday in 1951, I asked my dad why he spent so much time in the outhouse on Sunday mornings. This sparked a conversation that proved to be very informative.

He replied, "I do my weekly planning in that old outhouse. It's a place of solitude where I can do some serious thinking".

"Thinking about what"?

"What I might do for my customers or how I might acquire new customers. I'm in the business of selling various types of insurance, so I have to know who my customers are – or who they might be."

I said, "It seems to me most of your customers are tavern owners".

"Not necessarily, but we do have a lot of taverns in this town and taverns require certain special kinds of insurance."

"What do you mean special kinds of insurance?"

"People who sell liquor can be held liable if one of their customers consumes alcohol in their establishment and then injures someone else or damages their property."

I thought about that for a minute and then said, "So, if Bomber Pearlman gets drunk at Weaver's tavern and then gets in his car and smashes into Abigale Hanson, Mrs. Hanson could sue Mr. Weaver?"

"Possibly Paulie, but the laws are complicated and they can vary by state."

"What if one of Mr. Weaver's customers does something stupid, you know like Bomber Pearlman did last winter when he took his clothes off and jumped into the lake? He did it on a dare, but he did it after consuming a number of beers at Weavers."

Dad thought for a moment and then said, " That's probably not Mr. Weaver's fault. He wouldn't be held liable. No harm was done to anyone."

"Oh yes there was. The pastor's wife, Mrs Casper, was walking along the lake front and saw him crawl out of the lake, naked. She's been having trouble sleeping ever since."

"Really, I hadn't heard that." Dad was trying to hold back a laugh. "That is kind of funny, isn't it."?

"Yeah dad, it is. Is Kojecs's tavern one of your customers?"

"Yes it is."

"Well dad, I overheard one of Mr. Kojec's customers saying Kojec was better than a psychologist in diagnosing his customer's mental problems. He told Jimmy Baker to deal with his depression by getting a job working in highway construction. Said the fresh air and physical labor would clear his mind and get rid of the depression. Jimmie got the job, works 45 to 50 hours a week and spends his overtime earnings at Kojec's."

"You know what, dad? Maybe he could listen to Mrs. Casper's problems, you know have her describe what she saw when Mr. Pearlman climbed out of the water. "

"No, no Paulie. We're getting way off the subject here. I'm trying to explain to you how I plan my work week. I organize the tavern related businesses into one category and the rest of my customers into what I call, All Other. The All Other category covers retail food and clothing stores. You might call them the non-drinking group or the moderate drinkers. These folks are hard working, honest, church going and generally spend money on insurance."

"Would Mrs. Casper fit into this group?"

"Yes, why do you ask?"

"Well, I think you might help Mrs. Casper deal with her depression. You know, maybe introduce her to Bomber Pearlman or Mr. Kojec. It might help her to see Bomber with his clothes on. This would, at least, give her another image to carry in her mind. On the other hand, maybe she likes the naked image of Bomber, and this is why it keeps her up all night."

"That's enough Paulie, I don't want this brought up again. I've explained to you what I do in the old outhouse on Sunday mornings. I plan my work for the coming week. My planning covers my sales promotion activities, and I split it between taverns and their customers and the All Other category.

"I think you need another All Other Category dad for people who go to the taverns and can't keep their clothes on."

"Paulie, that's enough! These people are good citizens who sometimes make mistakes. So, let's not make fun of them. Now you know how I plan my week."

"All right, all right dad, But I'm not the one who jumped in the lake naked and it wouldn't bother me if I saw Mr. Pearlman without his clothes."

RED APPLES, RED WALLS, AND A BASEBALL BAT

People often don't know they are learning when they are learning. Years later a light bulb goes off, and understanding permeates the brain. There were a number of situations like that in my life. One involved a small investment that led to a business relationship, another a kitchen painted red, and finally a debt collection technique.

During the great depression, people often had to beg to put food on the family dining room table. My family didn't have to do this. We lived with my mother's parents in a four bedroom home on the north side of Lake Zurich, Illinois. Having a place to live with my grandparents took care of our housing costs and, in essence, helped finance my dad's insurance business. So, let's get on with the situations.

One day in 1938, dad was raking the front lawn when Charlie Mionske walked up the road between the the lake and our house. He said to my father, "Webb, I'll rake your lawn if you'll give me an apple off of your apple tree".

Dad agreed and Charlie finished raking the entire lawn. Dad gave him an apple and two one dollar bills. Charlie said, "That means everything to me, thanks Webb".

This was the beginning of a friendship that lasted for years. Charlie became one of the town's premier builders. Dad helped him with his insurance needs, often advancing premiums when Charlie was short of cash. Charlie Mionske was always a man of his word and repaid my dad whatever he owed him. Later on in college, I thought of this situation and realized how a small amount of invested dollars (plus an apple) can help provide the economic stimulus needed to start a business.

One day in 1951, Billie Best said to me, "Paulie, I'll pay you $10 to paint my kitchen". She was my mother's best friend, they had worked together at Kemper Insurance back in the 1920's . Billie was a widow with a teenaged

14

daughter. They were part of our "family" and, after the custom of the day, I called her "Aunt Billie". I agreed to do it, $10 was a lot of money in 1951. I showed up at Aunt Billie's home the following Saturday morning with several gallons of white semi-gloss paint. Aunt Billie said, "Oh no Paulie, I forgot to tell you I want the walls to be red semi-gloss".

"Red semi-gloss walls" I yelled! "Red semi-gloss walls.!" I had painted before and knew that painting over white with a clashing or different color like red, plus white ceilings, made the edging very slow and tedious. The job might take several days.

I said, " You're sure you want these walls to be red"?

"You betcha honey. Red will be "beumcifull". This place will be a real whoop de do."

Aunt Billie was still a 1920's flapper. She was a' whoop de do' in her own right.

So I began painting using Aunt Billie's red paint, hoping I could finish the same day. I finished late Saturday evening and when I got home told my mother and father about the red walls.

"Red semi gloss walls," my mother yelled! I had inherited my mother's red wall reaction. But the longer term lesson learned was that the customer is always right – even if she wants red walls.

One day, also in 1951, my dad said, "Get your baseball bat and come with me. "What for", I asked. "Bob Burnham owes me some money and I want him to see I mean business."

"Are you suggesting I hit him with a baseball bat?"

"No, no. I just want you to go with me so that he sees I mean business."

"I don't like this, dad. What if he doesn't pay? Then I have to hit him with the bat.?"

"No, you're reading too much into this."

"I'm not reading anything into this. You want me to hit a guy with a baseball bat. What if he has a baseball bat, then we'll have dueling bats."

"Nothing like that is going to happen, Paulie. I won't let it get out of hand."

"How did you get into this mess?"

"Well, you know that my customers are sometimes short of money. Rather than let their insurance coverage lapse, I pay their premiums. Later on, when they have some money, they reimburse me. Nobody in this town has failed to pay me except Bob Burnham. Nobody! What really infuriates me is he goes to several of the town's taverns and buys rounds of beer for the house. He's bought beers for everyone in town, and I can't collect what he owes me for advanced premiums. You want to go to college next year? That's your tuition money being pissed down the tavern's toilets."

I'd never heard my dad that angry and he got my attention with that tuition remark. So I went and got my bat, and we were off to Bob Burham's house. Webb Runkel and his enforcer Big Paulie (Big Paulie was 5 foot eleven and weighed 140 pounds). We pulled into the Burnham's driveway and dad got out of the car. "Just sit here and make sure anyone in the house can see that baseball bat."

Dad strode onto the Burnham's front porch and knocked on the door. Mr. Burnham opened the door and let dad into the house. They both disappeared inside. I sat there holding the bat up near my chest. I was nervous, to say the least. I tried to think like a mob enforcer. I thought how I'd feel if I was going to hit someone with a baseball bat. It occurred to me I'd feel safer if I had a machine gun. But then, I thought, the other guys might also have machine guns. After about five minutes, the door opened and dad came out with a fist full of cash and a big smile on his face. He got in the car and I said, "Is that next year's tuition money?"

He said, "Probably. And don't ever mention this to your mother. And we will never speak of this again. Understood?"

I nodded my agreement. I had to admit this had been sort of fun, scary but fun. I learned that borrowing money was a serious decision. You are going to need a plan to pay back your debt or you might have to face some kid with a baseball bat.

To summarize , the economics of opening a business involve start up money (or apples), identifying your customer's preferences (even red walls) and a workable plan to pay off your debts. These three situations had small consequences at the time but involved important long term economic principles.

FARMAN'S RESTAURANT

First I heard a crash, like the sound of something heavy falling, followed by a scream and the scraping noise of furniture moving across the floor. As I entered the smaller dining room, I saw one of the diners fly backward and land on a table. The table collapsed from his weight and smashed flat onto the floor. His companion picked up a chair and swung it at him with one hand. The man on the floor rolled away and jumped up, fists clenched.

I had been working at Farmans for several weeks in the summer of 1955. Everything had been calm and enjoyable until this moment. I had been trained to handle my job, which was busboy. My job was to clean the dirty tables and set them with a clean table cloth and silverwear, make sure the condiments were on the table and that there was a glass of water for everyone.

Mr. Farman and his son Guy Junior, were great to work for, and gave me a lot more information than I probably needed. But, I appreciated it. For example, they explained how I could expect different levels of diners on any given night. Weekends, of course, were the busiest followed by certain holidays. On really busy nights, I sometimes had to go back in the kitchen and help the dishwasher keep a supply of clean knives, plates, forks, spoons and glasses Much of Farman's business coincided with the Arlington Race Track season and this meant the summer months were unusually busy. The race track was the main reason they needed a full time bus boy.

They also gave me a short course in customer relations. Guy Jr told me, "Just watch my father". I did and saw a master at work. He spoke to everyone who came in and called most of them by their first name. He was always available If anyone had a complaint or question.

It seemed to me we had covered all the bases and that most of our duties revolved around keeping the customers happy. So, what could go wrong?

Plenty. As I cleaned several tables that had emptied, I noticed two large guys at a corner table in the smaller dining room. As I cleaned one of the tables near them, I overheard, "If you'd let me bet on that big brown horse, I'd have won two hundred bucks"!

"Hey, I ain't your mama. You place your own God Damn bets!"

As I worked, they kept drinking and talking louder and louder. More people came in and Mr. Farman seated them at the tables I had just cleaned. I moved on into the main dining room and began to clean some more tables. As Mr. Farman walked by I said, "There are two guys in the small dining room who might have had too much to drink."

He replied, "Thanks Pauline," and glanced into the smaller room and walked into the cocktail lounge area and picked up the telephone.

That's when I heard the scream and saw the table collapsing on the floor. The two men were swinging wildly at each other. One swung and missed, his fist bouncing off the wall. The other guy, who had a large tattoo on his forehead, punched him in the face. Blood ran out of his nose, Bloody nose picked up a chair and threw it. It bounced across a table of food splattering liquids and mashed potatoes onto the floor. Tattoo face kicked him in the groin.

Mr. Farman yelled, "Push these tables around them, keep them in the corner."

The two men ignored us and kept swinging at each other. Another chair flew through the air and hit the ceiling chandelier. Chunks of glass rained down on the combatants.

The front door opened and Police Chief Prehm burst into the room carrying a night stick. He waded in between the two fighters and rapped each one of them on the head. They both went to their knees. The chief hand cuffed each of them before they knew what happened. Chief Prehm and several customers helped the two stagger across the street to the police station.

The fight was over. We never found out exactly what caused it – probably excessive drinking. Guy Junior said to me, "I've been helping my dad for15 years, and I've never seen anything like that."

Chief Prehm suggested to the two fighters that they never appear in Lake Zurich again. As far as I know, they never did.

GAMBLING

State troupers stormed Lake County in a massive raid with warrants charging that gambling was permitted from July of 1965 to January of 1966. Seven area establishments were hit in a day of lights, cameras and action! A total of 65 people were arrested in the county and charged with a variety of minor crimes coming under the heading of "Keeping a Gambling Place".

The people running the gambling places were local business owners. Their gambling games included jar games, punch boards, parly cards, lotteries, pinball machines, dice games and book making. Lake Zurich's mayor was charged with misconduct and official misconduct for permitting this to go on. He faced a possible five year prison term and up to $3,000 in fines.

I grew up in Lake Zurich twenty years earlier, in the mid 1940s, and experienced some of Lake Zurich's gambling on a personal basis. With my dad's permission, I played a few punch card games for a nickel a punch. After losing four nickels in four days and having to go without a coke on those days, I decided the odds of me ever winning were not very good and I'd rather have that nickel for a coke or a Baby Ruth Candy Bar.

I then was allowed to play the slot machines at Farman's Hotel and restaurant when there for dinner with my parents. I was again using my supply of nickels from my allowance and lawn mowing business. My experience with slot machines has made me leery. Invariably I started off winning modest amounts and then slowly but surely lost my winnings and eventually ended up down a dollar or two. Since I saw gambling in town during the mid 1940s, that meant it took county officials at least 20 years to begin legal action. When they acted, it took 20 minutes to swoop in and arrest 65 residents.

So as a youngster, I gambled under the close supervision of my parents as did other kids. Of course, we weren't playing with enough money to fund a lifestyle of dissipation. I kept track when I was ten years old and for the year I lost a total of $2.80. $1.75 of this was money I lost to my grandma playing rummy at the kitchen table. Grandma was an excellent card player. She always seemed to know what I had in my hand and played accordingly. After playing her for a year or so, I began to win at least as much as I lost.

Several times I jumped out to an early lead and grandma would decide that this time we wouldn't play for money. She spoke excellent English but would lapse into a combination of English, Swedish and slang.

"Paulie, ain't it lucky ve didn't bestellda (Swedish slang for betting) no money"

"Grandma, we always bestellda money." Bestellda was her swedish slang for betting.   But, getting back to Lake Zurich's travails twenty years later, It seemed to me the residents of the county were penalized for playing games of chance at a low dollar level. Probably low enough to ignore. It's hard to draw the line as to what is too much gambling and what is a safe amount, an amount that allows for games of chance without getting into dollar amounts that people can't afford. On the one hand, punch cards and jar games seem innocent while on the other hand, the involvement of book makers seems excessive.

The Lake Zurich business owners were mostly charged with knowingly keeping a gambling place. Several were fined $20 (not a huge amount even in the 1960s) and several had the charges dropped for lack of evidence.

The mayor's case was harder to define. Remember, he was charged with official misconduct. The case against the mayor was eventually dropped on the grounds the indictment was not specific enough to let the mayor know what he was charged with. In other words, what is official misconduct as it pertains to gambling.

If my grandma were still alive, she wouldn't have been confused. She would have said, "The mayor didn't bestellda no money".

People Who Are Neighbors, Volunteers, and In Touch With Heaven (and Hot Summer Nights)

PAUL RUNKEL

OLD MAN BAKER

As the old man bent over and grabbed the weed, his dirty gray fedora flipped forward as it fell and bounced on the dry ground. He leaned forward and grunted as he retrieved the hat. He was slender, about 5 foot ten inches tall, dressed in dark gray pants and shirt. I didn't recall ever seeing him in any other clothing. Old man Baker rented a small, one bedroom home on the church property next to my boyhood home in Lake Zurich, Illinois. After retrieving his hat, he continued to slowly and deliberately walk to his house. He walked up the porch steps, hung his hat on the ragged corner of a broken window shutter and entered through the screen door that made a scraping, banging noise as it closed.

I don't recall anyone calling him by his full name, not even the pastor of the church – he was always referred to as ' Old Man Baker'. The church property had a small chapel and numerous cottages that were used for revival meetings. Mr. Baker took care of maintaining the property for the church. I never saw anyone other than Old Man Baker enter or leave the run-down house near our property. I wanted to say hello to him, but my parents insisted that I not bother him. However, my parents would often share our holiday and weekend meals with him. My mother and grandmother were a little afraid to go over to his house, so my dad was always elected to carry a large portion of our food on a paper plate to Mr. Baker's house.

Sometimes I would see him standing in front of his house looking out over Lake Zurich. He was still as a statue – only occasionally moving his hand to wipe an eye. I often wondered what he was thinking. He seemed mesmerized by the lake.

One summer day when I was ten years old, I was putting together a sling shot using a v-shaped piece of a tree limb and a rubber strip cut from an old tire inner tube. I was standing near our property line and having trouble attaching the rubber strip to the wooden handle. Old Man Baker was using a push- operated lawn mower near our property line and he stopped to look at what I was doing. He had never appeared to notice me before and I was a little afraid of him. He took the slingshot and without saying a word looped the two ends on the y-shaped wooden handle. He picked up a stone, loaded the sling shot and fired. It slammed into a tree about 50 feet away – inches from a squirrel's head. The squirrel jumped toward another branch, missed it and fell to the ground, then scampered away. Mr. Baker handed me the sling shot, nodded his head and smiled showing a row of tobacco stained teeth. He began to push the mower and walk away from me. That was the longest encounter I ever had with him, and he lived next door to us for several years.

One Saturday the next fall, I woke up hearing the occasional scrape and banging noise of a screen door. It would scrape, bang and there would be several seconds of silence, another scrape , bang and more silence followed by the murmur of voices. I got up and looked out my second floor bedroom window overlooking the church property. There were some important looking men walking in and out of Old Man Baker's house. His screen door opened with a scraping noise, two men carried a stretcher out the door. There was someone on the stretcher. I raced down the stairs and found my parents and grandparents talking.

Dad gave me a hug and said, " The pastor of the church found Mr. Baker lying face down on the kitchen floor. He hadn't been seen for several days so the pastor checked in on him. Apparently, he has passed away ".

I was sad, remembering how he had helped me with my sling shot. But after a period of time, I forgot about him as did the rest of my family.

It seems the older I get, the more childhood incidents I remember. This one is disturbing. It bothers me because he appeared to finish his life with no friends or family around him. And we didn't really know anything about him. No one used his first name – he was just ' Old Man Baker,' not Charles or Tom or Fred Baker, just 'Old Man Baker.' Many folks, including mine, say he rejected their attempts to be friendly but it seems we could have tried harder. He was somebody, somebody more than just 'Old Man Baker.'

HOT IS SOMETIMES GOOD

I learned some valuable lessons in my childhood when it was too hot, too hot to sleep in my bedroom, so I slept on a cot in a screened in porch on the front of our home. Whatever breeze came across the lake into our house, I was the first to feel it. My parents would stay up longer and sit in the living room discussing some of the day's events. Their voices drifted out through the front window and usually lulled me to sleep. But on certain occasions, I heard a name or word that interested me. Then I stayed awake and listened.

One hot evening in 1947, I heard the name, Babe Ruth. He had died that day. My dad was telling my mother how astounding his home run statistics were - 60 in a single season and 714 for his career. Remembering my parent's discussion those many years ago, reminds me how important statistics are to the baseball fan. I am disappointed in today's stars who added to their numbers by cheating – taking steroids. It is interesting to note that Henry Aaron is the only player to break the Babe's lifetime record without using steroids. Only Roger Maris broke his single season record without the use of steroids. At least, it appears that way.

On another warm evening in 1950, I heard my mother's tone of voice become angry as she spoke of the international film star, Ingrid Bergman. Bergman had become pregnant with a child fathered by the Italian film director, Roberto Rossellini. Her husband, Peter Lindstrom, was unaware anything was going on. My mother and other folks of Swedish decent were furious with her for setting such a bad example for Sweden. She was even denounced on the floor of the US Senate. Today people seem to accept this kind of behavior as normal. Governor Schwarzenegger fathered a child while married. The problem was the mother wasn't his wife. Maybe he just got confused. Now we have Simon Cowell fathering a child with the wife of one of his friends. Again, there was probably some confusion involved.

Finally, one oppressive evening in 1949, I overheard my parents discussing the case of Philadelphia Phillies first basemen, Eddie Waitkus. A mentally unbalanced girl named Ruth Ann Steinhagen invited the ballplayer to visit her at the Edgewater Beach Hotel. When Eddie entered her room, she shot him with a rifle. The bullet lodged near his heart but he survived the attack. He returned to the major leagues but was never the same player. My dad commented on the situation by saying, "Maybe he just wanted to see if the girl needed help", to which my mother replied, "he was not the good Samaritan, he wanted a little free' you know what.' I actually wasn't sure what my mother meant but was afraid to yell out, "What do you mean"? I knew that if my parents were aware I was listening, their discussions wouldn't be so frank and revealing. Eventually I figured out what she meant by a little "free you know what".

This sad tale was the basis for a book that, in the early 1980s, became one of the best baseball movies of all time (my opinion). It was called, "The Natural", and starred Robert Redford. Redford plays Roy Hobbs, a ball player who is shot by a girl in a hotel room and is out of baseball for many years. He returns to the game in his mid- thirties and astonishes the baseball world with his talent.

Situations I heard discussed on that dark front porch many years ago, repeated themselves in my adult years. What is really interesting, is similar current events are treated so differently from the events of 60 years ago. Babe Ruth's home run totals were sacred for many years. Their importance has become diluted as several players, who achieved higher numbers, apparently enhanced their skills by using performance enhancing drugs (PODs). Ingrid Bergman's dalliances, once important enough to anger a part of the US government, are no longer very important. And what about Eddie Waitkus and Roy Hobbs? Weren't they expecting, as my mother put it, a little "free you know what."

In my opinion, baseball players who take PODs are cheating. Ingrid Bergman and Arnold Schwarzenegger were cheating on their spouses. Eddie Waitkus and Roy Hobbs cheated on themselves – they took actions that shortened their careers. The 1940s and 50s were comparatively innocent times. Can you imagine the ruckus President Clinton and Monica Lewinski would have caused in 1950?

We've come a long way since the times I evesdropped on my parents discussions on those hot summer nights .Baseball is not the dominant sport it once was. International film stars routinely have children without ever considering marriage. People today are more forgiving of the dalliances of the rich and famous. But I wonder what my mother would have thought about a little "free you know what" in the Oval Office.

VOLUNTEER FIRE DEPARTMENT

Would Lake Zurich support a volunteer fire department? The residents believed they would, so the first volunteer Fire Department was formed at a local tavern meeting in 1933. Over the years, the volunteers fought a variety of fires from homes and churches to businesses and peat bogs.

They started operations with two wooden, horse drawn carts. Soon they were able to attach the wooden horse carts to a Ford Model T truck. A new fire truck was purchased after several years of operation. Early fire fighters were called to a fire by the sounding of a bell. The nearest phone to the station was across from the fire hall. When a call would come in, someone would run across the street and sound the bell. In 1934, the bell became a siren. By 1938 a code was used, three blasts of the siren meant the call was in the village, five blasts meant it was in the country, and one blast signaled a potential drowning.

The firemen were responsible for raising much of the funds to finance their operations. The most popular fund raiser was the annual summer carnival. All the net proceeds went to the volunteer fund for maintenance and operations. Rides, gambling games, and water fights were popular activities. Featured rides were a merry-go-round, a Ferris Wheel, and an Octopus. Gambling included Big 6,darts and bingo.

Water fights were competitive between the local villages Five fireman from two villages faced off against each other with a barrel in the middle. At a signal, each side would start their water. When they drove the barrel past the other team, they won the fight. Water sprayed everyone who stood near the street. Of course, the kids loved getting wet. Teams were eliminated when they lost. The final two undefeated teams faced off on the carnival's final night for a championship trophy

The ladies' auxiliary operated a food tent that served the popular sandwiches and home made pies. And, of course, there was the ever popular beer tent.

Dances were another popular way to raise money in the in the 1930s and 40s. The fire department held its first dance on May 25, 1934 in Ivanhoe, Illinois. Admission was 40 cents for men and 35 cents for women. Later, the department held dances in its own garage.

The carnivals and dances were popular social events. Note the comment by Harold Reese, a long time village resident and business man. "My great joy was being a member of the Volunteer Fire Department. The department provided many social events and a close association of members who were very dedicated to the purpose of saving lives and property."

Over the years, many home and business fires were contained saving thousands of dollars worth of property. Two large fires were out of hand and the buildings were lost almost before the fire department was on the scene.

One occurred on December 20, 1942, when the Saint Matthew Evangelical Lutheran Church north east of Lake Zurich burned to the ground. Fire departments from Lake Zurich, Long Grove, Libertyville and Mundelein were called to fight the fire. They used all the wells and cisterns in the area and could not stop the conflagration. The fire began in the belfry in front of the building. The open belfry acted as a draft to draw the flames through wall partitions and the ceiling. When the fire burst into the open, most of the church was ablaze at once. Apparently, the fire was caused by faulty wiring.

Another area fire destroyed an entire boys camp building next to Honey Lake in the Biltmore section. My dad found out about the fire just after the fire department did. He said to me, "Come on, let's drive over there and see if we can help". Honey Lake was about three miles from our house. As we neared the Lake, we could see flames shooting into the dark sky. I could recognize the fireman in the fire's light. The acrid smell of burning electrical wiring made me cover my nose. I tried to see through the black smoke. The Fire departments from Lake Zurich and Barrington were already on the scene. My dad said, "This is awful if boys are in that building".

One of the Lake Zurich fireman said, "There don't appear to be nobody in the building, Webb." And there wasn't. The building and the camp were open to various groups of boys all year long ,but no one had rented it for this time period. So, while property was lost, lives were not.

Peat moss fires were a constant problem. Peat bogs were an accumulation of decayed vegetation. They could burn undetected for periods of time. They fueled global warming and were a hazard to human health. They were creeping ground fires, and fire departments had to deal with them during the dry periods of the year.

At one such fire, the department did a walk through the field extinguishing the fires they found. They were particularly looking for underground fires. When they completed their walk- through, they took a head count and found they were missing Dud Geary. They quickly doubled back and found him trying to crawl out of a large sinkhole. Peat bog fires were not as dramatic as flames shooting out of a several story building. But, they could be just as dangerous to humans.

As world war II dragged on to the middle 1940s, mock air raid drills were practiced under the direction of the fire department. At a signal using the fire department siren, all lights in the village were turned off – a complete blackout. Lights in every home were turned off, no light that could provide a target for the enemy was allowed to escape from any building. American communities were concerned about the long range missiles Germany successfully fired at England. If they could hit Great Britain, the next target would likely be the United States. Communities around the US believed it was best to be prepared.

My dad was an air raid warden, which meant he wore a special helmet and checked his assigned area for any escaping light or noise. He walked the several blocks on the north side of the lake checking each building. It was an exciting time for kids. We couldn't wait to see all the village lights near or on the lake flicker off and the entire town go pitch black. It became dark and quiet. No cars moved, people turned off their radios and spoke in whispers. The only sound I heard was the lapping of waves against the shores of the lake.

From 1933 when the volunteer fire department was formed to the 1950s, the department became an efficient fire fighting group. They went from horse drawn hose carts to modern fire trucks. Fund raisers over the years helped finance operations and keep the department up to date. The fire department's activities provided a social life for the residents while protecting people and buildings.

BUD FARMAN AND THE BIRDIES

I was racing through the halls of Ela-Vernon High School to get to my last class of the day. I passed through the glass paneled door that led to the first floor class rooms. I was about 20 feet past the door when I heard a crash, the breaking of glass and the tinkle as the glass hit the floor. I heard someone cry out in pain, I turned to see my friend, Bud Farman, sink to his knees holding his arm. He had pushed his arm through one of the door's glass panels.

Bud was taken by ambulance to a Waukegan hospital where surgery was performed on a cut tendon in his left wrist. The doctors told his parents he would need a lot of exercise to rehabilitate that wrist. The first bit of good news for Bud and his parents was that the doctor was an avid golfer so he recommended that Bud take up the game. He believed swinging a golf club would strengthen the tendons in that wrist. Bud's dad bought a membership at Biltmore Country Club, and his avocation as a golfer was underway.

My dad and mother were good golfers and taught me to play when I was seven years old. So now I had a golf buddy at Biltmore, and the two of us played frequently. By my mid teens I was shooting around 90 for eighteen holes. Bud was terrible. In the beginning, he couldn't break 120. But he was determined to play the game well. He and I played frequently. When he had no one to play with, he played by himself. He had a bag of golf balls and spent hours on the practice range after he took lessons from the local pro.

By the time we entered college, Bud was a 15 handicap, frequently scoring in the high 80s. One day he said to me, "One of these days I'm going to beat you".

And one of those days he did. By our mid college years, he was beating me as often as I beat him. At this point, we were both 8 handicaps and frequently scoring in the high 70s.

During the summer after my sophomore year, I got a job at Farman's Hotel and Restaurant. Since Bud and I worked the same hours, 5pm to midnight, we played golf all day until 5 pm and then went to work in the restaurant, then home to bed and up at eight am to play golf.

One day we decided to hold a Lake Zurich Open championship. It was open to anyone whose parents lived in Lake Zurich and had a membership at Biltmore – So this so- called "Open" included Bud Farman, Jack Rakow and myself. As we drove to the golf course, Bud kept saying he was going to get a birdie and win the tournament. We were racing down Honey Lake Road, gravel and dust flying around the car, when there was a loud thud, something hit the front of Bud's car. He slowed to a stop and we saw a bird impaled on the hood ornament.

I remarked, "That's the only birdie you'll get today"!

Bud laughed and said, "No, that's an omen. I'll get a lot of birdies today"!

Bud and I were tied for the lead as we teed off on 18. We both reached the par five green in three and had uphill, side hill, 30 foot putts. Jack was six strokes behind and he putted out. I hit my putt to within two feet and putted it in for a par. So it was up to Bud. If he makes the putt, he wins. If he misses we are tied and have a playoff. He hit a putt that looked good but then appeared to be going past on the high side. At the last moment, it broke severely left and dropped into the cup for a birdie and the win!

Bud shot 79 that day. He had come a long way from that kid who shot in the 120s six years earlier.

After college, we went our separate ways – Bud running his father's hotel and restaurant and I working for Montgomery Ward in Chicago. We managed to play several rounds every year. Every trip to Lake Zurich meant a stop at Farmans' for a dinner or a drink. But our lives changed dramatically as we entered the 1990s. Both Bud and my first wife died of cancer.

By 2014, my second wife and I had moved to Florida on a part time basis. One sunny day in December of 2014, I was driving past one of the many Florida golf courses near our home. Around the holidays, I often remember the people from my past. I thought of Bud and how much he would have enjoyed retiring to Florida and playing golf all winter. Something dark flew at my windshield , then hit the front of my car. Thud! I'd hit something. I stopped, got out of the car to check the front end. There was a dead bird stuck in the grill.

Some will say, "What a coincidence"!

I don't think so. I think Bud Farman was telling me, "Don't worry about me, Heaven is full of great golf courses."

PAUL RUNKEL

Trailblazers

The Development of the Dial Telephone, the Summer Theater,
a Builder Extraordinaire, and Two Fine Teachers

PAUL RUNKEL

GRANDPA CHARLIE AND THE TELEPHONE

Grandpa Charlie's life began a long way from Lake Zurich, Illinois. His story began on the Erickson family homestead just outside of Lindsborg, Kansas, in 1869. My great grandfather and great grandmother settled there after a move from Varmland, Sweden. My grandpa, Charles Erickson, and his brother, John, began their life's work in a wooden workshop on their father's farm around 1880. The boys were creative and spent hours in their workshop. They watched their father perform difficult tasks using simple equipment and then began work on their own projects.

Grandpa Charlie said they were influenced by the worldwide move towards automation. They had many irons in the fire including a printing telegraph, a new way to create sound from a phonograph, and an automatic piano player. They also considered creating a horseless buggy. The engine functioned but wouldn't generate enough power. The inventors were young and confident, believing they could create anything if they worked long and smart enough.

Their creative spirit continued to challenge them. Their workshop was a busy place both day and night. The Erickson brothers were influenced by their friend, Frank Lundquist. Frank worked for the Chicago Telephone Company for six months and then returned to his home in Lindsborg. He visited a hotel in Salina,Kansa where he observed the operation of a telephone exchange. Frank shared his ideas with John and Charles. It occurred to them that someday these connections between phone lines could be made automatically. Charles wrote, " It could be handled using the same principles as the printing telegraph we had underway. We realized this could be a goldmine if we could perfect it. So we put aside all other projects for the time being."

By late 1892, they had completed a model of a telephone exchange that had a capacity of one hundred contacts or lines. John and Charles decided it should be presented in Chicago. Financial support was hard to obtain but they opened a workshop using an old store front. Toward the end of 1893, A. E. Keith and A. B. Strowger of the Automatic Telephone Exchange Company contacted the Ericksons. According to Grandpa, "Their equipment didn't work as well ours".

After several hours of discussion, the Strowger people became enthusiastic supporters of the Erickson's . They admitted that the Erickson brothers' equipment was advanced compared with theirs. The result was that they made a proposition for John and Charles to join their company. This new agreement took place in December of 1893. The brothers were on their way to creating a new system. They advertised it as the "Girl-less, cuss- less and wait- less telephone". The Erickson's telephone system required fewer lines resulting in the reduction of jobs and shorter wait times when making a call.

The most dramatic contribution in telephone systems from the Ericksons was the dial telephone. It was based on the finger wheel. Dialing a number wound up a spring. When the finger was withdrawn, the tension in the spring caused the dial to return to its normal position. An oversimplification would be; winding to the number nine required 9 clicks, the number one, one click, etc.

The brothers continued their association with the Strowger Company until 1901 when the Automatic Electric Company was formed. John and Charles became development engineers with the new company. The engineers remained with the electric company until they retired in 1931.

Grandpa Charlie purchased a summer cottage on Old Rand Road in Lake Zurich in the 1920s. He converted it to a year round home in 1931 and spent his retirement years living there. My parents and I moved in with grandpa and grandma in 1938.

John and Charles Erickson, Frank Lundquist, A. B. Keith and Almon B. Strowger shared in the development of a great industry. Their automated dial system was used around the world for over 50 years. The Erickson Brothers were credited with 150 patents.

Grandpa Charlie also had a way with words. At a testimonial dinner given for the brothers in 1939, he talked about the early days and the conversion to automation that took place in their workshop.

"A sheltered nook in the Smokey Valley of central Kansas, today preserves the crumbling and forgotten monument to the dial model that substituted brains and iron fingers for the human young lady . In this nook lies the remains of our workshop, the building that cradled the birth of the machine girl. Forgotten that monument may be, it lingers on in the sweet memories of the two who began their work between those walls."

CHARLIE MIONSKE

Many men don't live long enough to see their visions of the future come true. Charlie Mionske saw part of it before his untimely death.

Charlie was one of LakeZurich's builders during the expansion that took place after World War ll. He also saw that the population increase would continue well into the future.

Even as a child , he was a risk taker. He left home at nine years old to find his dad who had left the family home in Crown Point, Indiana. His dad had moved to McHenry, Illinois, several months earlier. Charlie had enough money to buy a train ticket to Palatine, Illinois. He got off the train and started to walk to McHenry, about 30 miles north. He got as far as the Kropp farm on the outskirts of Lake Zurich. The Kropps gave him food and a job.

While there, he took the name Charles Kropp and became part of the family. He was Lake Zurich's gain and McHenry's loss. He worked on the Kropp farm from the time he arrived until the age of 16 when he signed up for the Civilian Conservation Corp (CCC), and was sent to Wisconsin to build and work in the camps that the government was establishing. He learned some of his building skills at these camps.

While on the Kropp farm, he built and sold birdhouses to earn extra money. His daughter Lori says, "I find that touching. As a little orphan boy he lacked his own home, yet built homes for birds and later homes for families".

Charlie attended school only through the fourth grade. Lori again remarks , " I find this amazing. I have read some of his letters of appeal to the village with proposals for change in the zoning laws, they are indeed in his own hand writing. His reasoning is clear, and grammatical construction mostly correct".

In 1934, he met and married his wife Caroline. On the day they were engaged, he said to Caroline, "You're about to marry Charles Mionske".

"Mionske!" She exclaimed. "Who is Charles Mionske?"

Charlie explained, he thought he should revert back to the name on his immigration papers.

As his daughter Lori remarked, "Things were different back then".

Charlie grew to love Lake Zurich and over time became a builder of homes. In his 30 years in this field, he oversaw the development of three subdivisions. He worked hard to provide fine homes, plus the required shopping and civic improvements needed in the town. True builders make the community a better place than it was when they arrived on the scene. Charlie certainly did that.

As the second World War went on into the mid 1940s, the army needed more men. Even though Charlie was in his 30s and had five dependents, he was drafted and assigned to work in Fort Leonard Wood's kitchens. He served until late 1944 when he was discharged as a Corporal.

He became one of the town's leaders serving as commander of the American Legion Post. Recognizing the value of a free press in every community, he invested in a local newspaper. Charllie ran for mayor in 1945 against Herb Wesner, Ela High School's principal. Charlie campaigned on a platform that proposed the town prepare for the coming economic and real estate expansion. He believed Lake Zurich had to grow to stay alive. Herb and his followers wanted the town to stay small and comfortable. Wesner won by a large margin of votes.

Charlie concentrated on his construction business. He worked hard and played hard. He would voice his opinion to whomever would listen. "Some people in this town got their heads up their asses, they don't see the economic expansion that's coming. We already got a new factory and more will come. New businesses need workers and workers need places to live."

Eventually, Charlie was proven right. Take note of the following comparison. The United States current total population of 323 million represents an increase of 2.3 times from the mid 1940s. Lake Zurich's population, during the same time period, has increased to 20,000, an increase of 20 times.

Charlie opened a second subdivision between the railroad and Route 12 near the seawall. Mr. Jensen owned property at the lake's outlet on Old Rand Road. He tired of the overflow running through his property so he blocked the traditional outlet. The lake's water began to rise and threaten Charlie's subdivision on the other side of the lake. His response was, " Open that outlet or I'll dynamite that f...ing dam." Mr. Jensen's reply was, "I'll shoot anyone who goes near that dam." Eventually, cooler heads prevailed. No one was shot or dynamited. Other solutions were found.

In 1953 Charlie again ran for mayor, this time against Anton Kuchman. Charlie still represented the townsfolk who wanted to expand the village.

He lost, but continued to fuel the expansion by building new homes for people who demanded them.

Charlie began suffering breathing problems in his early 40s. In the morning, Caroline would find him sitting up and asleep in a living room easy chair. He found it easier to breath if he remained upright. He was not building anything at this point in his life. He spent his time in real estate development and politics. Finally, he relocated to Florida with Caroline and their youngest son Robert, where he was more comfortable living on the beaches of the Gulf Coast.

He returned to Lake Zurich in 1959, in order to have a series of tests on his heart at St Theresa Hospital in Waukegan. All the tests showed his heart to be healthy. The next day, he suffered a heart attack. Charlie drove himself into downtown Lake Zurich and pulled into Luerssen's gas station. He got out of the car and collapsed. He was carried to Dr. Pessis' Office across the street, where he died.

Charlie's rival newspaper published an obituary that included these remarks, "A giant among pygmies who looked to him for leadership. Charlie made the wheels turn – without false pretense. Tough, shrewd and bluntly outspoken, Mionske fought for what he believed – with no holds barred. No other single person in the history of Lake Zurich had the effect Charles Mionske did on the growth of the village. Small in size, Mionske cast a long shadow across the community he called his own."

There is an over used cliché about people of vision, they say he was a man "who lived ahead of his time". Charlie Mionske was a man of vision "who lived IN his time".

THE LAKE ZURICH PLAYHOUSE

When is a teacher a mentor? When she not only teaches but acts as a counselor, a tutor and a big sister all rolled into one. Chicago's Goodman Theater had several performers who fit this definition. These young folks were looking for ways to fill the demand for live entertainment and provide learning opportunities for the Goodman students. People had radios and movies, but little or no live shows or stage performances in the early 1940s. Some locations in northern Illinois and Wisconsin filled this need for summer theater programs. One of these locations was in Lake Zurich, Illinois.

Several performers and teachers from Chicago's Goodman Theater decided to open a summer stock program in Lake Zurich. Actually doing this was not a simple proposition. Money was scarce, the country was just coming out of the great depression, and available funds were being used to finance the entrance into the Second World War. Would the founders be able to start a theater from scratch?

Bella Itkin, the leader of the group, was a newcomer on the Chicago stage. Bella brought with her Sidney Breeze another Goodman teacher and student. Their initial goal was to find young, talented performers who wanted to increase their understanding of the craft.

And find them they did. They found young performers like Geraldine Paige. Geraldine made her acting debut at the Lake Zurich playhouse in the early 1940s. She graduated from high school in 1942 and entered Chicago's Goodman Theater School. She and other students helped organize the Lake Zurich summer program. Geraldine went on to become one of the most important actresses of the 20th century. She was regarded as a mastercrafts women who could bring out the innermost detail of the character she was playing. She appeared in 28 films, 16 Broadway plays, and innumerable TV and radio programs.

Another notable Lake Zurich actor who went on to star in many venues was Harvey Korman. Harvey was born in Chicago and attended the Goodman Theater School before becoming a part of Lake Zurich's summer theater. Harvey played a wide variety of characters during his career., but his most memorable roles were regular performances on the Carol Burnett TV Show.

Lois Nettleton ,Miss Chicago in 1948, attended the Goodman Theater school and appeared in a number of Lake Zurich roles. Lois went on to appear in numerous stage, screen and TV productions.

Lee Richardson was another Lake Zurich and Goodman School actor who went on to perform on stage, film and TV. His career lasted for over four decades.

Another of Dr. Bella's students was Tony nominated Kevin Anderson who wrote, "She was an outstanding teacher who gave me the confidence to believe in myself. If you saw Dr. Bella as the lights went down and the play was about to begin, you would see this look of complete joy and passion come over her face."

With talented performers and effective leadership, word got out that some great entertainment was provided at the Lake Zurich Summer Theater. So the audience came from all over northern Illinois . Most were from Chicago's suburbs, particularly the north shore. Many in the audience were from Lake Zurich, both residents and vacationers. A fun night out was dinner at Farmans then on to the evening's performance.

The theater was located on Main street across from the sea wall and the lake. It consisted of two cottages connected together to form the structure with, seating of about 200 people in graded seats including proper lighting. The connecting area had no second story and formed most of the theater . The carpenters were skeptical , but went ahead with the design provided by the drama company. It worked and a theater grew out of two attached frame bungalows.

Numerous plays were performed over the years. Here is a sampling from the early to middle 1940's:

"Vivacious Lady"

A romantic comedy based on the 1938 film starring Ginger Rodgers and Jimmy Stewart. It was love at first sight between a college professor and a night club singer.

"The Drunkard"

A play written in the early 1800s. It was arguably America's most popular play before "Uncle Tom's Cabin".

"An Ideal Husband"

An Oscar Wilde comedy revolving around blackmail and political corruption. Wilde's main point was that no one should be entirely judged by their past.

The actors and the set crew found the theater provided in depth training in dramatics and basic living skills. In addition to acting and set design, the performers learned to build sets and provide meals for everyone involved in the productions. Much of what the actors learned came from their back yard rehearsals. Idyllic best describes the rehearsal site behind the theater and under a huge oak tree. The company found the spot inspiring as they rehearsed mornings and afternoons. Rustic furniture was dragged out to be used as part of the temporary stage while the auditorium was being prepared for the next show. Three chairs together became a couch, a short bush a floor lamp and a certain tree, was a door to another room. Even a rock had a preassigned role.

One play required a telephone call. The director would yell, "Ring,ring."
The nearest actor picked up the rock, "Hello! Yah, this is Johnny. (Pause) I'm fine. How are you Mrs. Sterling?"
If the rehearsals were not going well, a visit from Dr. Itkin would motivate the cast to become fully engaged. She would deliver suggestions like, "Murry, make your character more believable. While you deliver your line, walk over to the ashtray and snuff out your cigarette. Walk behind Helen so that you don't block her from the audience, she has a line to deliver as you approach the ashtray. Remember these are real people with real mannerisms."
So, the training and motivation of an actor was covered by the theater's founder and other Goodman personnel. Was the demand for entertainment satisfied by the program? Yes it was. The audiences were presented with a series of performances that illustrated some of the best writing available in the 1940s. Dr. Itkin and other Goodman performers proved that theater can be entertaining when performed by actors who are just learning their craft.
While the Lake Zurich theater ended it's run in the early 1950s, summer theater is still available in certain Midwest areas . More importantly, there are a number of year round, semi professional and amateur productions produced by several of the Chicago area park districts and schools. Three of the better known are the Lake Zurich Performing Arts Center, the Schaumburg Theater Program and Palatine's Cutting Hall. For an evening of fun, go to one of these shows and realize the performers are presenting a work of love and passion. Dr. Itkin will be looking down from above and smiling.

HARRIET AND MEL

Teachers exposed us to the outside, adult world. How they acted toward us, and each other, was a learning experience. Our teachers were motivated toward success, and they encouraged us, corrected us when we got out of line, and told us when it was time to start acting like the young adults we were, not the young kids we had just been.

All the Ela-Vernon teachers were role models. Harriet Jacquat and Mel Eide strongly influenced my thinking and, for purposes of this article, represent all the the teachers in Ela-Vernon High School in the early 1950s. They provided examples of what you could become if you earned a college degree. Still, I was not convinced I should go on to college. Earning money right out of high school was an attractive alternative.

Miss Jacquat graduated from high school in Normal, Illinois, where she was a state ranked tennis player. She went on to Illinois State Normal University . Then she earned a masters degree in Biology from the University of Wisconsin. She came to Ela-Vernon in the mid 1940s and taught biology. She stayed at Ela until she became head of the biology department at Stevenson High School during the seventies. Mr. Eide arrived in Lake Zurich in 1932 after earning a masters degree. Mr. Eide began his career teaching Special Studies and music. He was also the band director. On the athletic side, he coached the freshman-sophomore basketball teams for 25 years, and the varsity baseball teams for a number of years. The baseball teams won six Northwest Suburban League titles under his direction. In 1946, he was named Assistant Principal of the school. He was promoted to Principal in the late 1950s, a position he held until he retired in 1968.

Miss Jacquat and Mr. Eide didn't just teach us subjects, they taught us how to learn and succeed. One day in class I asked Miss Jacquat to clarify a certain biological principle. Her reply was, "Paul, if you had done your homework and prepared for class, you wouldn't have to ask that question." She was teaching us how to learn by being prepared to discuss the day's subject in class.

Another learning experience took place for me in a baseball game against Palatine High School. I was playing on the team and not hitting very well. I kept getting called out on strikes. Finally, Mr. Eide called me over and said, "You can't outguess the umpire and his calling of balls and strikes – particularly when you have two strikes on you. In this situation, it's better to choke up on the bat and get ready to swing at anything close to the strike zone. Just put the ball in play, make the other team have to field the ball. The more they have to field the ball, the more errors they will make. That's better than just standing there with the bat on your shoulder waiting for a pitch you like. So if you have two strikes, get ready and if the pitch is close to the strike zone, swing at it."

In a game against Barrington, we had the lead and Barrington was up to bat for their last at-bats with one out and a runner on first. I was playing shortstop. The batter hit a ground ball back to the pitcher, the pitcher whirled and made a perfect throw to second base. Both our second baseman and I had started toward second base but we saw each other and stopped. No one was covering second base and the pitcher's throw went into center field. Instead of a game ending double play, Barrington had runners on first and second with one out. Barrington eventually tied and won the game. Mr. Eide called me over and said, "You're in charge on that play. Before the pitcher pitches to that batter, you decide who will cover second. In this case, you should cover second because the Barrington batter was left handed so you would be playing closer to second. In any event, you've got to decide before the hitter bats." This was another situation where I was being taught to plan, to think ahead.

Teaching was Miss Jacquat's passion, and relationships were her love. She maintained contact with her peers, her students, and their parents throughout her life. She provided financial assistance to individuals and organizations in both the Lake Zurich and Bloomington- Normal areas .Mr. Eide was active in his church where he sang in the choir. He also was president of the local Lions Club for several years.

I was walking down the first floor hall, near the end of my senior year, when Miss Jacquat stopped and asked me where I was going to college. When I didn't answer her question right away, she said, "You'll do well if you think, question, and prepare for class. Remember"? She smiled and moved on. Another day in early June of that year, I was walking down Main Street in Lake Zurich when I saw Mr. Eide on the other side of the street. He waved and came over to wish me good luck in college. He said, "Go out for the baseball team, you'll make the team Pauline. Try out, work at it, mentally prepare for the games and play hard."

Those were the last two encounters I had with Miss Jacquat and Mr. Eide. I didn't realize it at the time, but high school teachers would have an enormous impact on my life. I'd like to turn the clock back and thank Miss Jacquat and Mr. Eide – and all the other teachers at Ela-Vernon High School.

College seemed easier and within reach the more I thought about it. When teachers like Miss Jacquat and Mr. Eide say you can make it, what other motivation do you need? I went to college.

PAUL RUNKEL

War

The Beginning of World War 2, Escaping a Sinking Ship, Surviving as a
Prisoner of War, and the Heroics of an Air Force Flyer

PAUL RUNKEL

DECEMBER 7, 1941

Swinging on a tree rope with Peter Earling, I could see the lake glistening in the bright sunlight across the road from his home. As I swung higher and higher, I felt like I was going to fly out over the lake. Peter was swinging almost as high, and a feeling of exhilaration made us laugh hysterically.

I yelled, "you can't swing as high as I can"!

"Yes I can." Peter yelled back!

It was a warm winter's day in Lake Zurich, Illinois, warm enough to wear a light jacket and to smell the moisture of the lake. I was six years old and Peter was a year younger. His family had rented a home four doors west of ours on Old Rand Road, which runs along the northern border of the lake. We were becoming good buddies even though my mom was not fond of his mother. Peter's mother liked to stay in her pajamas all day long – pajamas that were always various shades of red, some solids and some plaids. My mother didn't approve of this. She believed people got up, ate breakfast, got dressed, and went to work or cleaned house, or went to school or went outside and played. I thought lounging in pajamas during the day was a great idea, particularly if it was raining.

As we were swinging back and forth this Sunday morning, Peter's mother came out on the front porch - in her pajamas - and said, "Paulie, I think you'd better go home and talk to your parents, something terrible has happened; the Japanese have attacked Pearl Harbor." It was December 7, 1941.

I quickly started for home, wondering what a Japanese looked like. I also wondered where Pearl Harbor was, then I remembered. There was a "Harbor Something" down the road from our house. Now I was scared. We could quickly drive to that Harbor Place in my Dad's car. That meant they were close to us. I began to run as fast as I could, afraid to look back, a

Japanese could be chasing me! I heard footsteps behind me, I ran faster. I tripped over a tree root falling hard on my stomach. Got up, my heart pounding, and continued to run, finally reaching our yard. I was gasping for air. I raced up the steps through the back door into our home.

My parents had already heard the news. My father said, "Don't worry, Pearl Harbor is thousands of miles from here." And my mother added, "You don't need to be afraid, go back outside and play." So, I calmed down and went outside. But, I sensed my parents were concerned so I worried and was a little afraid.

When I'm reminded of World War II and Pearl Harbor, I remember the Earling family and their tree rope and how one moment Peter and I were flying high and then, all of a sudden, I was scared and running for home as fast as I could. The most vivid memory of the first six years of my life is that Sunday morning in December of 1941.

I have detailed memories about where I was and what I was doing when I heard an airliner crashed into the Twin Towers on 9/11, and when my wife called and told me President Kennedy had been shot. But, my most vivid historical memory is when Mrs. Earling came out on her porch and told us the Japanese had bombed Pearl Harbor. Her pajamas were red.

MICHAEL CHARNOTA

The aircraft carrier Wasp had just provided support for the US invasion of Guadalcanal. The Wasp replaced carrier losses incurred near Australia in the Solomon Islands during the September, 1942 battle of the Coral Sea.

Michael Charnota, a Lake Zurich businessman, stood on the carrier's deck and looked over the vast sea. He remembers enjoying the warm sun and wishing he could remove his shirt. He thought, "We've got it easy, the Marines on Guadalcanal are fighting in the steamy island climate. I was glad to be aboard a ship". At 3:20 PM, a Japanese submarine began firing torpedos at the Wasp. In a matter of minutes, three of them hit the carrier.

Michael says, "That's when all hell started."

The first struck the gas tanks. The second and third hit the ammunition storage area. The power went out and this was followed by a muffled thump and a huge explosion. The decks were engulfed in flames. Black smoke billowed from below decks. Michael choked on the acrid smell. He covered his nose with his shirt. It was chaos, hundreds of men clamoring over the side of the deck.

Michael says, "You didn't have time to be scared." He looked over the side of the ship and saw men jumping from the deck into the water 65 feet below. Others grabbed the water hoses and slid down. Charnota grabbed a water hose and worked his way down. Michael comments, "65 feet was too high to jump."

Everyone fought to get to safety; swimming, swallowing water, kicking – all desperate to avoid drowning. Some yelled to each other, some were screaming. Charnota swam as fast as he could. He got to a life boat and, with a grunt, pulled himself up and onto it. Once his raft was full, the men tried to paddle away from the stricken ship. They were surrounded by water burning where the carriers' leaking gas had caught fire.

Michael thought, "This must be what hell is like."

Several of the men were singed by fire, but they were able to paddle past the burning water to safety. They drifted for what seemed like a day,but after only about three hours they were rescued by a destroyer. Michael began to shake with fear as he remembered the dangers he'd faced over the past several hours. Images of men jumping from 65 feet high into the water, immediately disappearing forever. Some surviving the jump and swimming through burning gasoline to safety. Two hundred of his shipmates failed to survive the disaster.

For years after, the thought of his friends lost in the sinking of the Wasp tormented him. In his later years, he began to be able to deal with those memories. He received a large framed picture of the sinking from an Esquire Magazine photographer. He was "thankful " to get a copy.

Michael Charnota came home to the United States and received a 30 day leave of absence. He returned to active duty when he joined the U.S.S Essex and the Pacific Fleet for 18 months. He then completed his four years of service at the Navel Armory in Chicago.

Men who survived the loss of the Wasp are sailors who became living memorials to the sacrifices made by WWII Naval personnel. One such survivor is Michael Charnota.

HAROLD GIESE – PRISONER OF WAR

A US Battalion Executive Officer looked out of his bunker on December 15, 1944. He saw cone shaped evergreens standing in deep snow. The snow sparkled with crystals and formed a scene of beauty. He took a deep breath, savoring the crisp, clean air and retreated into the bunker where he again read the latest intelligence report.

"The Germans in front of us have only a handful of beaten and demoralized troups supported by two pieces of horse drawn artillery."

Actually, hiding in that beautiful forest was a huge force – the battled-hardened ISS Ranger Corp. As the German attack began, the US troops stood around and admired the thunderous artillery display thinking they were hearing US guns. They were not. As some of the US troops began to be cut down, the others dove for cover in their fox holes. Artillery fire rained down on the GIs. Harold's unit and several others, were overrun by the experienced Germans. The US forces were taken by surprise. Harold's unit was quickly surrounded by the German troops. The German officers gave the Americans two choices. Either surrender or be annihilated . The US force surrendered. American bodies already littered the fields.

Harold's company was marched away from the fighting. They came across the bodies of two Americans propped against a tree that was broken in half. Their heads were blown off and nowhere to be seen. Harold's unit was part of a large US surrender on December 19, 1944 They were marched off to the east, their hands clasped on the tops of their heads. One US writer described it as a "river of humiliation" . They bedded down in piles of straw and were not fed for days. Eventually, they were loaded onto French railway cars. The Germans had used this railroad to transport cattle, the floors were covered with manure. The GIs were packed in tightly.

Harold's legs felt like they would collapse, but he was packed so tight he couldn't fall down. The stench was pervasive Some men experienced overpowering feelings of claustrophobia, they screamed but couldn't move..

The long, slow freight trains were ideal targets for US P-47 fighter bombers. The American pilots continuously raked the unmarked trains with machine guns and rockets. Many Americans and Germans died in the attacks. At one point, the train stopped and some Americans jumped off and found protection near a cliff. Harold and others stayed on the train. But some bombs hit the cliff and started an avalanche. Many of the men from Harold's car were buried alive. Harold escaped injury and possibly death when later the same day, a rock flew through a hole in the train car's roof and hit him in the head. The rock bounced harmlessly off his helmet. Harold said, "The helmet saved my life." The helmet had already protected him during the combat before he was captured, when two bullets bounced harmlessly off his head.

The trip continued and the men began to hold daily prayer services. On Christmas day, they received food - buckets of sorghum. The men continued to pray and thank God for His blessings. The day after Christmas, they found piles of straw alongside the tracks. When the train stopped, they gathered the straw and used it to sleep in, and to clean out the railroad cars.

After ten days, they arrived at Stalag 4b, a large British Prisoner camp. They received hot showers and a bowl of soup. They moved into barracks where they had their own bunks and a central stove.The prisoners were now under the rules of the Geneva Convention and, hopefully, would receive better treatment.

The men began to receive food parcels from the Red Cross. A warm bunk and mediocre food seemed like luxurious living to these prisoners. Soon they were sent out on daily work details. Their work project was to dig new railroad track beds for German freight trains. They worked from 6 AM to 5PM. Officers yelled instructions at them in German.

Harold said, "No one understood them and no one really tried. "Somehow, it became known that Harold could speak some German. So he was made a "straw boss" to relay the orders from the officers to the men. "When I couldn't understand the officers, I would tell them, but sometimes I would order the men to do something else. This got everything in a fine mess. But we didn't care. Pretty soon the men would only work when they felt like it. After they found out they could get away with this, they worked less and less."

As the war neared its conclusion, most of the guards were old men. One of them was 60 years old. He yelled at Harold constantly because he thought Harold understood German. "But he talked so fast," Harold said,

"I didn't understand him and I didn't care what he said at this point."

One day Harold blew his top and told the old man, "Americans are getting close, when they free us I'll find you and slit your throat." He scared the old guy and had him apologizing for an hour. After that incident, the old man did little yelling."

At this point, Harold got the guys together and told the German Officer off. Then they began to shovel one shovel full of dirt an hour. Rumors flew through the camp that the Americans were closer and closer. Russian troops were also getting close to the POW camp. Air raids in the area were becoming more frequent. When the air raid siren went off, the men stopped working and took off for the air raid shelter. They usually stayed in the shelter until quitting time.

The Americans began wandering to a field near the camp that was full of German troops. They exchanged various items of food and bartered for other goods. The night before the Russians were expected to arrive, the guards marched the Americans away from the camp and toward the approaching American troops. The Germans knew they would all receive better treatment from the GIs. They tried to walk fast, but were quickly exhausted. Many fell to their knees, got up to plod on away from the German camp. They took turns carrying those who couldn't walk.

Then they saw the American troops. Harold said, "It was a joy I had never experienced." The men were taken to field hospitals for physical exams and a good meal. After this they boarded a plane for England and more complete physicals. They ate, got pills, shots, and more medication. The trip home across the Atlantic was uneventful. But when they passed the Statue Of Liberty, emotions ran high. Harold says, "Never was a sight so beautiful, particularly when a short time ago, you had no idea you'd live to your next meal , much less return to the United States."

JAMES OBENAUF

Twenty minutes past Amarillo, Texas, in a SAC bomber, Lt. James Obenauf heard an explosion and felt the aircraft shudder. His plane was on a training flight out of Dyess Air Force base in June of 1958. Jim observed the right wing was engulfed in flames. The aircraft commander and pilot, Major Graves, gave the bailout command twice over the interphone. He and Lt. Cobb parachuted, unhurt, through the bottom escape hatch. Remaining onboard were Major Maxwell and Lt. Obenauf. Jim tried to exit the plane by activating his ejection seat. He pushed all the buttons several times but it wouldn't activate, except the canopy over the cockpit flew off in preparation for the ejection. Lt. Obenauf prepared to follow Major Graves through the bottom hatch but found Major Maxwell had not exited, he was unconscious and blocking that escape hatch – probably from lack of oxygen. The 3x4 hatch was too small for both of them to climb through together, and he couldn't open Maxwell's parachute. The good news was the fire in the damaged engine had died out.

So he would have to attempt the impossible, fly the plane down at 450 miles an hour in freezing temperatures with an open cockpit. He climbed back into his pilot's seat. First, he lowered the plane's altitude to 15,000 feet providing oxygen for Major Maxwell and himself. Then he contacted Sweetwater Air Defense Radar Station. They kept Lt. Obenauf on course until he could connect with the Dyess Air Force Base Tower. He wanted to attempt the landing at his home base, Dyess, because he was most familiar with that landing field. Sweetwater was able to keep him on course, and kept him apprised of his progress, helping him to know when he was not keeping the plane level.

While Obenauf flew steadily back to Dyess, the officers and crew on the ground prepared the landing data Jim would need to bring the plane down safely. The ground crew was not optimistic, the major problem was the open cockpit. There was a bulkhead in front of Jim's pilot seat. He had to lean out to the side to see where he was going. The wind and sand would be blinding. The base commander remarked, "It was hard enough to land a plane from the rear cockpit under normal conditions."

Jim's narrative that he provided to his commanding officers included the following remarks; "On the trip back to Dyess, I experienced moderate to severe turbulence and caught myself in 40 to 50 degree banks, at times the plane was almost out of control.

"Ground Control Administration, {GCA), lined me up on final, but I couldn't hold any heading since I couldn't make out the air speed indicator. GCA advised ne I was too far left. I couldn't go around because I couldn't see the landing strip anymore. And I couldn't see the air speed indicator. I was flying final approach by feel , so I made up my mind the only thing to do was to go on in.

"I hit the ground and pulled the brake chute. After that all seemed normal, I shut down all electrical systems. Immediately after stopping, I cut all the remaining engines and gingerly climbed out of that live ejection seat."

It was a picture perfect landing as Jim brought the plane to a stop at the end of the runway. He and Major Maxwell were hospitalized and treated for shock, frost bite and burned eyes. They were released in several days and soon returned to active duty.

Jim was awarded the Distinguished Flying Cross for his heroic efforts to save Major Maxwell and the damaged B-47. He remained in the Air Force for 16 more years serving in the air war portion of the Viet Nam conflict. In 1974, James Obenauf retired with the rank of Lt. Colonel.

PAUL RUNKEL

Sports

Undefeated in Conference Play, In Basketball and Football, The Reign of
Baseball as the Number One Sport, and Golf as a Lifetime Game

PAUL RUNKEL

ELA'S MAGICAL SEASON

Several hundred people were yelling, cheering, and stomping their feet as the players on the two teams raced back and forth on the basketball court. They shot the ball from right under the basket, up to 40 feet away. When Ela scored, the gym would rock with cheers and applause. The din was so loud I could hardly hear myself think.

Then, cheerleaders would whip the crowd into an even greater frenzy. "Rah, Rah, Sis Boom Bah, Ela High School, Rah, Rah, Rah."

I was 10 years old and my dad had taken me to my first high school basketball game. I loved it.

I had never seen anything like it and before the first half was over, I was asking my dad, "Can we come to next week's game? Please! Please!" It was the beginning of the 1944-45 season and I didn't fully understand how special this Ela team was. We were a small school (about 150 students) and the varsity team included five boys from the Grever family. All were related as brothers and cousins. Kenneth and Orville were brothers. They played forward. Their cousin, Herman, was the center. Herman's brother, Lloyd, was one of the guards, and cousin Glenn was the manager for the team.

Ela won the game that night, but I don't remember the score. The win moved them four games into a magical season. Before the season started, Ela was ranked forth in the Northwest Suburban Conference behind Bensenville, Palatine and Barrington. But so far, Ela had not lost a conference game. Unless you've played team sports at the varsity level, you don't understand how difficult it is to remain undefeated in a well - balanced high school athletic conference.

So, this was my introduction to high school basketball. As I've grown older, I've realized my favorite type of baskeball is the "old game" where the tallest player on the floor was 6' 4" and there were no slam dunks. The offense would move the ball around the floor with short, crisp passes as they looked for the open man. Sometimes teams would use an effective fast break involving two or three players. A quick pass to midcourt after a rebound followed by several short passes leading to a layup basket.

In 1945, the first Ela vs. Bensenville contest was at Ela's gym. Ela's coach Warfield had scheduled special practices for a week prior to meeting the Bisons. On the day of the game dad said, "We're going to the Ela game tonight, they're playing the best team in the conference".

We got to the game just as it started. Something didn't seem quite right. The game seemed to be played in slow motion, particularly when Ela had the ball. The Ela players would bring the ball up court with a series of slow passes, and then they would dribble around for a minute or two. At one point, it took them five minutes before they took a shot (there was no shot clock in the 1940's). They seemed to be waiting for the perfect shot. Ela rarely missed because of their shot selection.

The Bensenville crowd began to get angry and booed Ela's slowdown tactics. The Bensenville players didn't know how to react to the deliberate, ball control strategy. It seemed to be working because Ela held on to a one or two point lead throughout the game and finally won a nail biter, 18 to 15.

As the season went on, Ela continued to win and reached the final conference game of the year with 13 wins and no loses. The last game was against Bensenville on their court. Ela had clinched the conference championship but wanted an unbeaten season. My dad and I drove to Bensenville and arrived at game time. The Bensenville fans were already booing our team in anticipation of another slowdown game.

Bensenville took the first shot. The ball bounced high off the rim. Herman Grever grabbed the rebound and fired a pass to Kenny Grever at mid court, Kenny whipped the ball across the court to Orville Grever who two handed a bounce pass to Lloyd Grever, who drove to the basket for an easy layup. Ela led 2 to 0. Ela continued their fast break game which surprised the Bensenville players and allowed the Bears to get ahead by as much as 10 points. Bensenville recovered their poise and made a game of it. But Ela was too quick and controlled the defensive boards. Ela won 39 to 34 and had a 14 game undefeated conference record.

Baseball had been my game for several years. But I now had another favorite sport. I probably attended 90 % of Ela's varsity basketball games over the next seven years. I will always remember the noise and excitement. There is nothing like a tight game, an Ela player lofting a high set shot, the ball drifting down and swishing through the net followed by an explosion of cheers. Those sounds and scenes are an indelible part of my memory.

GOLF, NOW AND ALWAYS

Pushing the tree branches aside, I peered unto a large field and could see a man swing a stick and hit a small white ball. There were three other men who did the same thing. I was five years old and had wandered through the woods behind our home until I could see one of the fairways of the Lake Zurich Golf Club. I was fascinated.

One of the men swung his stick, and I heard a click followed in a few second by a whack as the ball slammed into one of the many trees that lined the fairway. Another second or two went by, and I heard a string of short, unfamiliar words. They appeared to have three or four letters each. I went home and said, "Mom, Mom, there are some men in the woods hitting small white balls with sticks. If the ball hits a tree, they yell damn and duck". She got a horrified look on her face and said, " They weren't saying duck. Do not say damn and duck together."

"What's wrong with duck?"

"Never mind, I'll explain when you get older. Don't pay any attention to those men. They are just a bunch of stupid, old golfers."

Golf has been an important part of my life. I've played golf, watched golf and worked in the golf industry. My relationship with the game started in the woods on that day in 1940.

I grew up in Lake Zurich, Illinois, living in a home that overlooked the lake from our front porch. In the rear, about 200 yards behind our property, were two of the fairways of Lake Zurich Golf Course, a private club that had been built way back in 1895. The club was exclusive. The membership consisted of about 40 wealthy men from Chicago," stupid, old golfers," according to my mother .

In a couple of years when I was seven years old, my dad, an

accomplished golfer, took me with him when he went to practice at the golf club where he belonged. I learned the proper way to hold and swing the golf club. Sometimes, my father and mother would take me with them to play golf – my mother was also a very good golfer. They encouraged me to play the game telling, me it was a sport I could play all of my life.

So I played golf off and on through grade school and high school. I wish now I had worked on my game, but other things always seemed to get in the way. Baseball came first, then girls (or maybe it was the other way around). While I was a decent baseball player, I think I could have been an excellent golfer. In high school, one afternoon during the spring, there was no ball game or practice so the golf coach asked me to play with the team against Barrington High School. I played and won my match.

In college, I played on the varsity baseball team for three years and then quit to play on the golf team in my senior year. I had been working nights during the summer and playing golf all day. I had lowered my handicap to seven, but could not make the starting six players. I was ranked eight. That meant, the only way I would play in a team match against another school would be if one of the starting six, plus the seventh ranked player, could not play or was currently not playing well. This did happen once, and I played and won my match. So my limited high school and college golf career ended with two wins and no defeats. I guess that is something to be proud of but you can see why I feel that with some effort, I could have been much better.

As an adult, I played golf off and on but there were many years when earning a living and family took up much of my time. At the age of 52, I had lost my job and was starting my own accounting business when I got a call from a recruiter.

He said, "A Chicago manufacturing company would like to interview you for the job of Chief Financial Officer." I said, "No thanks, I'm interested in starting my own business." He said, "This is a company that manufactures golf clubs."

I said, "I'll have to think about it." Two seconds later I said, " I thought about it, when do they want to see me"?

So I worked in the golf industry for seventeen years before I retired in 2004. I have played a lot of golf over the past 20 years or so. My parents were right, it is a sport for your lifetime. I can't seem to get my handicap back down to a seven, but I can still play pretty well. I should be able to shoot my age in the next year or two. This is a big deal among the better senior players.

I think my dad would be proud of me, my scores are similar to his in his senior years. Would my mother be proud of me? In some respects, yes. She might be disturbed over one thing. When I hit a really bad shot, I might let loose with a barrage of four letter words. One day after a particularly poor shot, my playing partner looked at me and said, "Did you say mother duck?"

BASEBALL

Winning baseball was a Lake Zurich trademark. In the decades from 1930 to 1955, many of the records are incomplete. But, we do know that Ela High School won at least four northwest suburban conference titles during the 1930's. The local papers printed stories with bylines like "Foes Fear Ela Prep Nine".

A number of conference titles were won by Ela during the 40's and 50's. If Ela didn't win the championship, they were at least in contention. In the late 1940s, Ela had several of the best players in the northwest suburbs, players like Eddie Prouty, George Schwarz, Jerry Centoni and Mike Rizzo. Again, the local papers covered these young athletes and their exploits with articles like "Ela Favored In Prep Race".

If a player wanted to continue playing baseball after graduation from high school, Lake Zurich had a town team, the Lake Zurich Athletic Club. Many towns had their own baseball team and they competed against each other in the Shore Line League. Eddie Prouty and Mike Rizzo played for this team after their high school careers were over. Several other players joined Eddie and Mike on this team. I played for Ela High School and went on to play for the Lake Zurich Athletic Club. My value to the team was that I could play all the infield positions and hit maybe .200 to .250. I fit the description, "Good field, no hit." I felt lucky to be playing with some of these outstanding players.

In the mid 1950s, Lake Zurich's defensive alignment often looked like this; Catcher, Mike Rizzo. Pitcher, Eddie Prouty. First Base, Paul Obenauf. Second base, Augie Weber. Short Stop, Paul Runkel. Third base, Don Maxwell. Left field, Bill Bettis. Center field, George Radke. Right field, Marty Halverson.

Other pitchers included Elmer Dobner and a 35 year old pitcher who had spent a number of years in the St. Louis Cardinal's farm system. When he retired, he was pitching for the Cardinals triple A team. Unfortunately , we've lost his name. I do remember he won a lot of games for Lake Zurich. We usually played two games a week, and with our strong pitching, our opponents rarely scored a lot of runs. So we won many more games than we lost in the Shore Line League.

Local residents often wandered over to watch the Wednesday evening and Sunday afternoon games. A large crowd was 50 people, but keep in mind Lake Zurich's population was only 1,000 – maybe 2,000 if you consider the surrounding farming communities of Echo Lake, Forest Lake, Long Grove, and Buffalo Grove. One Sunday afternoon we drew over 200 people for a game against the Dr. Rex King All Stars.

In addition to the Shore Line League games, we played games against the Johnsburg Tigers, the Evanston All Stars and the Dr. Rex King All Stars. Johnsburg was one of the best amateur teams in the country. One of their players eventually made it to the majors. As I recall, they beat us rather badly .The Evanston All Stars were an all black team we enjoyed playing because they had lights on their ball field. In one game in Evanston, their clean- up batter hit a long home run off Eddie Prouty. The next time he came to bat, Eddie tried to move him off the plate with an inside fastball. The pitch got away from Eddie and hit the batter in his shoulder just inches from his head. For a moment we thought he would charge the mound and start a fight. But he thought better of it and trotted down to first base. An inning later, the game ended with us in the lead.

We gathered around our bench to get ready to leave for home. We noticed some of the Evanston players were pointing at us and arguing with their coach. Soon they were walking toward us in small groups. Mike Rizzo said, "Oh, Oh, we got a problem." They didn't look happy. But when they got to our side of the field, they smiled and shook our hands. We breathed a sigh of relief.

The Doctor Rex King All Stars were another all black team, this one from Waukegan. Doctor King was the owner and manager of the team. He was a local physician who loved baseball. His team played a number of teams in northern Illinois. They were a pretty good team but had weak starting pitching. Doctor King was an older gentleman who apparently was a good pitcher in his youth. So he made himself the number one relief pitcher. As all older men do, he had lost the zip on his fast ball. We loved to see him come into the game because, he had nothing to scare us with.

The first time I batted against Dr. King, he threw me a fast ball right down the middle. It looked as big as a grapefruit and I hit it solidly over the left fielder's head, probably the longest ball I ever hit. Thank you, Dr. King!

67

As I said earlier, we won a lot of games because we had good pitching. And, what goes with good pitching? Good catchers. Catchers are often the best athletes on the team. Squatting behind home plate for 100 pitches a game while catching a baseball moving toward you at 80 to 100 miles an hour is no easy task. Catchers also need strong arms and use them to slow down or eliminate the other team's running game. They reduce the other team's stolen bases either by, throwing them out when they attempt to steal, or by picking them off their base when they take too big a lead. One of the King All Stars could run like the wind. In our first game with them, he singled and then drifted a little far off of first base. He danced around first base and our pitcher made a couple of lazy throws over to first to keep him close. After the base runner was used to the slow rhythm of these throws, Rizzo called for a pitch out and, almost without looking, fired a throw down to first base. Our first baseman easily tagged the runner out. This has a way of slowing down the opposition's running game.

In my five years playing for Ela-Vernon High and the Lake Zurich Athletic Club, I played with three different catchers. All of them were good athletes . Chuck Wesner and Pete Altmann were the catchers in my high school years. Chuck and Pete also played on the football team. Mike Rizzo was both the manager and catcher for the Lake Zurich Athletic Club team. Mike also played football in high school. Mike was one of the better hitters on the high school and athletic club teams.

By the middle of the 20th century, baseball was established as America's game. It was a game men could play until they were well into their thirties. Other than the catcher, they didn't need special equipment. Some of the young men in the Lake Zurich area took advantage of the game's popularity and continued to develop their skills in order to compete against neighboring villages or, in several instances, to begin a professional baseball career.

ELA-VERNON FOOTBALL

In 1953, the first color TV was sold in the United States, Elvis Presley recorded his first song, Dwight Eisenhower was inaugurated as President, and Ela-Vernon High School won their first conference football championship.

I decided to come to my first homecoming at Ela-Vernon High School in the fall of 1953. The main attraction that year was the football team. They were playing their last game of the year and were undefeated needing one more win to win the conference championship. The opponent was Bensenville. I was anxious to see some of my classmates, we had just graduated five months earlier.

Strangely enough, I didn't see very many of them as the game started. But Bob Anson (a high school close friend and college roommate) was sitting high up in the bleachers on the 30 yard line. He saw me and waved me on up to join him. We exchanged hellos and back slaps even though we had just seen each other the day before at Lake Forest College. After joking around about "long time no see" we discussed how the team had remained undefeated through the first eight games.

The team looked nervous. They dropped passes as they practiced their short passing game. They kept looking at Bensenville warming up on the other side of the field. Coach Bill Lehman was yelling at them to concentrate, focus on what they could control. They quit looking at Bensenville.

Ela-Vernon's Bears seemed to channel that nervous energy as the game started. Fenner and Chaffin quickly scored touchdowns and we led 13 to 0 at the end of the first quarter. A couple of times we couldn't make a first down, and Chaffin got off two booming punts to set Bensenville back in their own territory.

But then Bensenville scored and the game was close at 13 to 6. The turning point came when Gudgeon scored on a 55 yard touchdown run. I can still see Danny start around our right end. As he cut down field, two blockers came out of nowhere and knocked down two Bensenville defensive backs. At that point, it became a foot race between Gudgeon and the Bensenville safety. Gudgeon won. It was 20 to 6. After that everything seemed to go our way. Ela-Vernon's front line line took over the game as they sprung Danny Gudgeon loose again on a touchdown run. Glen Chaffin then scored on a touchdown pass from Donny Prouty and we were up 32 to 6. All of a sudden it was halftime and it looked like we didn't have much to be nervous about.

Dick Price, one of the team's linemen, has told me about Coach Lehman's halftime speeches. "Coach Lehman's half time talks always had one same message no matter what the score. Boys, we want to play this second half as if the score is nothing to nothing." So, as usual, the team came roaring out of the locker room for the second half. The defense took over and Bensenville did not score another point. Tom Rorke scored a touchdown for us and the game ended with Ela-Vernon leading 39 to 6. Bob remarked, "That's cool, an undefeated season and a conference championship"!

I thought about the game on the way back to college the following day, There was a lesson to be learned here. There were great achievements outside of football in 1953. Color TV and great rock music from Elvis were the result of focused rehearsal. General Eisenhower became president in 1953, but he became a famous leader when he directed the 1944 D Day Landings of World War II. That landing was the result of months of preparation and practice. Coach Lehman used these techniques to enable Ela-Vernon to overcome nervousness and win the conference championship game.

EPILOGUE

You've read 21 stories about people, events and locations in Lake Zurich, Illinois. The stories illustrate living in the middle of the twentieth century. Actually, these people and events probably represented hundreds of small towns across the United States.

What can we learn from these stories? For me, it is that Lake Zurich provided an unusually large number of creative examples and situations that the kids could emulate.

People in Lake Zurich seemed to be going somewhere in a hurry. They did take the time to plan, using an abandoned outhouse in Illinois, and a wooden shed on a farm in Kansas. They fashioned a theater out of two summer cottages connected by an attached walk-way. They used simple tools and a basic understanding of electricity to not only create housing for the town's residents, but to provide the basis for a dial telephone system.

Some residents survived their military experiences to fight another day. Michael Charnota was rescued from his sinking aircraft carrier, Harold Geise lived through months of brutal captivity, and Jim Obenauf saved his SAC Bomber, a fellow flyer and himself from a deadly crash landing.

Athletic teams rehearsed, and used their brains to win conference championships.

Finally, there was The Lake – the center of attention for many of the town folks. If you wanted something to do, you could always go " Over By The Lake".

PAUL RUNKEL

EXPLANITORY REMARKS – THE LOCAL HIGH
SCHOOL'S CHANGING NAME

Ela High School opened its doors as a four year high school in 1929 (some records say 1925). In any event, it was named "Ela" after one of the township's first settlers, George Ela. The school remained "Ela" until 1950 when Ela and Vernon school districts merged to form Ela-Vernon High School.

The addition of Vernon township increased the number of students from 155 in 1950 to almost 300 in 1953.

This arrangement continued until the middle 1960s when several disagreements between the two townships could not be resolved. As a result, the Vernon residents developed their own school in Lincolnshire, and named it Stevenson.

The Ela residents retained Ela-Vernon's properties and the Lake Zurich location. The school was named Lake Zurich High School. It provided a four year high school for the village of Lake Zurich, and several smaller communities like Echo Lake and Forest Lake.

Today, the name of the school continues to be Lake Zurich High School.

PAUL RUNKEL

BIBLIOGRAPHY

14 Taverns and an Outhouse
- Paul Runkel's memories
- Mrs. Casper, Mr. Kojec and Bomber Pearlman are fictitious characters based on a number of residents living in Lake Zurich in the 1940's
- Most of the events described actually happened

Red Apples, Red Walls and a Baseball Bat
- The Runkel family memories and files
- The customer who would not pay his debt is based on a real situation. The collection by using a baseball bat is real. The name Bob Burnham is fictitious.

Farman's Restaurant
- Paul's memories, Bud Farman's memories

Gambling
- Frontier Enterprises Newspaper
- Paul's memories

Old Man Baker
- Paul's memories

Hot is Sometimes Good
- Paul's memories
- The story of Ruth Ann Steinhagen, who attempted to murder Eddie Waitkus, Philadelphia, Phillies first baseman, is on the Internet. It was written around the time of her death in 1983

Volunteer Fire Department
- Ela Historical Society and Museum files

Bud Farman and The Birdies
- Paul's memories
- Bud's memories

Grandpa Charlie and The Telephone
- Kansas Historical Museum

- Automatic Electric Company Newsletter
- Hazel Runkel, Vanlaningham file

Charlie Mionske
- Ela Historical Society and Museum files
- Lori Mionske, Shula files
- Mr. Jensen is a fictitious character based on people who lived through the real events

Lake Zurich Playhouse
- Ela Historical Society and Museum Files

Harriet and Mel
- Paul's memories
- Chicago Tribune Obituaries
- Ela-Vernon High Student Newspaper "Bear Facts"

December 7, 1941
- Paul's memories

Michael Charnota
- Ela Township Museum files

Harold Geise – POW (Prisoner of War)
- Ela Historical Society and Museum files
- Harold's daughter's letters to the Museum
- "Citizen Soldiers" by Steven Ambrose, chapter 13, pages 357 and 358

James Obenauf
- Ela Historical Society and Museum
- Austin Texas Library
- Albian Reporter News article
- SAC Combat Crew Magazine

Ela's Magical Season
- Chicago Herald American News
- Ela Historical Society and Museum
- Letters from Bob Snetsinger to the Ela Museum

Golf Now and Always
- Paul's Memories

Baseball
- Paul's memories
- Ela Historical Society and Museum

Ela-Vernon Football
- Ela Historical Society and Museum
- Ela-Vernon High School newspaper, "Bear Facts"

PAUL RUNKEL

ABOUT THE AUTHOR

Paul Runkel grew up in Lake Zurich during the 1930s, 40s and 50s. He attended Ela-Vernon High School and graduated from Lake Forest College in Lake Forest, Illinois. He spent most of his career in Financial Management with Chicago area companies.

Paul wrote and published a time travel story, "Time For Baseball", about an average major league baseball player who travels back in time to 1946 where he becomes a hall of fame performer.

Paul now lives in Huntley, Illinois and The Villages, Florida with his wife, Linda.

www.ingramcontent.com/pod-product-compliance
Lightning Source LLC
Chambersburg PA
CBHW071834020426
42331CB00007B/1727